Victor —
I hope the
year ahead is
filled with all
you deserve.
Karen 12/99

HALF PINT EDITIONS

Just Labs

PHOTOGRAPHS BY DALE C. SPARTAS
TEXT BY STEVE SMITH

WILLOW CREEK PRESS
Minocqua, Wisconsin

Published by WILLOW CREEK PRESS, INC.
PO Box 147, Minocqua, WI 54548

For more information on Willow Creek Press titles,
call 1-800-850-9453.

Individual poster prints of the photographs in this book are
available for purchase directly from the photographer.
Write to: Dale C. Spartas, P.O. Box 1367,
Bozeman, MT 59715, or call (406) 585-2244.

Library of Congress Cataloging-in-Publication Data

ISBN 1-57223-217-X

Printed in Canada.

Contents

Dedication

Dedicated to Donal C. O'Brien, Jr., who took me on my first duck hunt,
introducing me to the pleasure of knowing, owning (and being owned by),
and loving a lab; for to know one is to love one.
And to Buck, my first "luv-ador."

–D.C.S.

Acknowledgments

I would like to thank and acknowledge the following people who helped me with this project,
John Berger, Randy & Jo Berry, Anthony Carafa, Randy Carlson, Peter Corben, Marty Fischer,
Peter Gurney, George Kelly, Roger Keckeissen and Schook, Kim Leighton, Dave Maynard,
Kerry Malloy, Don O'Brien, Jr., Bill Owen, Pete and Tanya Rothing of Diamond R Kennels, John
Scott, Miles Ward, Jack Weiss and the North American Hunting Retriever Association (NAHRA)
and, of course, all the wonderful dogs,

–Dale C. Spartas

PORTRAITS

One Breed, Three Colors
Countless Personalities

T he usual suspects: Labs come in three colors, one breed, countless personalities. They are at once clowns, companions, confidantes, counselors, pets, protectors, and hunters. They seem at times to have their own agenda, yet never stray far from our side. They can carry an egg in their teeth and never puncture the shell, set it down gently, and then nonchalantly chew their way through a chain-link fence. They don't know the meaning of the word "fear," nor often the meaning of the words: "No," "Come," "Sit," and, "Stay off the furniture, you knothead!"

Some Labs look like puppies for only a few weeks, gracefully surrendering the things of youth for the adult world after an early career spent chewing slippers and door moldings, hall carpeting, and the good sofa . . .

... others never lose their puppiness. Even in the dignity of age, there's still the playfulness, the impish eyes, the manner that says, "If you really love me, you'll get down on the floor and wrestle with me. Right now."

O ld dogs, especially old Labs, are indeed something rare. I don't mean rare in that there aren't many of them – there are. But rare in the sense of, "What is so rare as a day in June?" Rare as in "remarkable," "singular," "irreplaceable," and "precious."

There is an elegance in age that is a bittersweet potion made up of equal parts savvy, shrewdness, serenity, and sweetness. They become so much more in tune with our moods, adjusting theirs to fit ours.

These old dogs, these old friends. There's a certain sadness, an emptiness that comes over us as we watch them dream by the hearth, doing the things again in their musings that they did once in their youth. The paws moving, the eyes flickering, the flews lifting in a barely audible little *woof* now and then.

This is their world now; and don't feel bad for them. We can only hope for pleasant dreams and warm hearths when the last of our best days, too, are but memories.

LIVING WITH LABS

Send in the Clowns

Labs are partners for life. They become a true part of the family, hitching a ride in the car, making sure you put in your five-K run every morning, and generally doing their best to run a tight ship. Their aging process seems to more closely parallel that of humans than other breeds. From exploring, hyperactive pups, each a seething cauldron of misdirected energy, they slide into a bull-headed adolescence, which sort of rhymes with nonsense. From there, they evolve into sage, experienced adults, and finally into doting old grandparent-types, grateful for attention and conversation.

Very few breeds will, for long, put up with the pulling, prodding, pinching, and the general bedevilment of kids. But Labs relish it, they seek it. They seem to know that these little characters are defenseless, and that there is a commonality there because the dogs are but children themselves.

S omeone once said that it's possible to train a Lab by treating him like a three-year old child; if so, then it's no wonder Labs and kids are so inseparable . . .

. . . Imagine a guardian who never really sleeps, one with the eyes and ears to rival the best security system ever devised, one that knows roads are bad things and will steer your youngster away from them. At the same time, they realize that a short little kid with an ice-cream cone is like a gift from God.

As a function of selective breeding, Labs are born with an overwhelming urge to carry stuff in their mouths. And for the most part, they aren't exceptionally fussy. It can be a dead fish, dead decoys, a dead thermos, or a wheel lug from a '54 Chevy.

It doesn't matter what it is, really, but if it feels like a game or it smells of food – or us – the item under consideration stands a good chance of being boosted up and toted about.

B ut oh, to hold a warm, fat game bird. Now there's something that tingles all the way to the genes. In the words of Dan Fogelberg, it's breeding and it's training, and it's something unknown.

PLAYING HARD

One speed and one volume control
– pegged all the way right

Plaguing the local tabby is an amusing diversion on a summer afternoon. Smart Labs know the exact size of the demilitarized zone that surrounds each house cat. The saber-rattling is impressive, but the actual border incursions are both rare and memorable.

A small child – the ultimate, marvelous toy. To a Lab pup, a child is for munching and licking and tormenting. To a child, a Lab pup is a set of sharp teeth in a tender ankle and a warm, wet tongue unerringly inserted into an eye socket or any available ear canal.

W hen the Game gets going, the game of, "I've got it and you can't have it," no other breed of dog has a chance.

And pups find themselves so outclassed, we wonder why they don't quit in despair. But, of course, your average Lab pup doesn't have any quit.

TRAINING HARD

*An athlete is only as good
as his coach*

The training of a dog that wants to please isn't a task, it's most often a pleasure. The handler/coach and the athlete/dog have their roles, and through repetition, each learns his. The object is to make the communication between the two constant and unbroken, despite distance and topography.

The handler must trust his dog, but he often can see things that the dog cannot, so the dog must trust the signals received from the coach. For Labs, play is fun, but they find some of their greatest enjoyment in training. They were born to work.

Their enthusiasm for the task at hand is boundless. When you watch good Labs work, you get the sense that they are muttering under their breath, "If only I could fly ... if only I could fly ... if only ... "

It's called fire or drive or intensity, and it is indeed all of these. But it is more. It's a poetic frenzy, a ballet of blood lines, one the dog does not understand but must dance until the time comes when he can dance no more.

Their drive to retrieve can only be slaked when a handler throws a dummy or hunter shoots a bird – for the dog. They take direction and cue from the human, and so the partnership is one of trust and respect and cooperation. The dogs respond to the whistle and to the voice and to the hands and praise of each "owner." These are the ways the connectedness is maintained, across the distance and the years.

Because they need human contact more than other hunting breeds to satisfy their drive, Labs are born with an innate desire to please. That's why they watch us, making eye contact, studying.

They're looking for the signs of what pleases us. The handler also needs the dog, so the affection that blooms between them is so natural that it is questioned by neither.

WORKING HARD

Training, Discipline, Dedication
The Lab as Athlete

R ibbons and medals and plaques mean nothing to Lab competitors. It is enough for them to be there, to do their best.

There is a subculture made up of folks who test and trial Labs. Some call it a game, though it's anything but. It is, for the most serious competitors, a business, a social structure, and a way of life. Only the best dogs win, and in this brotherhood of trainers, only the winners are bred to produce other winners. Thus is the breed enhanced. Even if a Lab never sees a test or trial grounds in his life, if the dog is a good one, most likely it has the blood of champions and near-champions coursing through its veins.

The tests can be simple for young dogs – pups and derbies – incredibly complex for the finished dogs. But these Labs are, in the most real sense, professional athletes. They have learned the art of grace under pressure and of doing their best on command. No other animal that competes, including the long-legged thoroughbreds at Churchill Downs, exhibits more heart and tenacity and guts than a field trial-bred Labrador retriever. Period. There will be no discussion.

The field trial subculture has spawned, like many such cultures, its own related economic infrastructure. There are trainers and breeders, suppliers of specialized equipment, customers for the stuff, authors and publications, and those who campaign another person's dog in exchange for money. The field trial game is big business, and those immersed in it have a vested and good-natured interest in the improvement of the product and the betterment of the breed.

T he weekends and the weeks and the years slip by in this field trial culture . . .

… because owning a Lab is a way of life. Like those who own horses or yachts or vintage cars, the culture overtakes you, and "you can't tell the dance from the dancer."

I t was probably at a Labrador retriever field trial that the term "top dog" entered the vernacular. You can't measure the heart and drive of both owner and dog that go into thirty-seven cents worth of silk ribbon. It is only at a trial – not the duck blind or the pheasant field – that we find the best of the best.

HUNTING HARD

*All that has come before
is but for this*

A t the molecular level, Labs are hunting dogs, there to help us round up a square meal, to bring back to us, undamaged, the makings of a game dinner, one they won't share except for the odd tidbit smuggled to them under the table. The exceptional nose, often underestimated in Labs, the wonderful eyesight, and the willingness to put all else aside in order to please their human – this is what Labs in the shooting field are all about.

A s hunters, Labs are the original versatile breed. In upland hunting, they function as flushers, not giving a bird on the ground an instant's rest until it takes to the air to find safety from the juggernaut bearing down, closing in. That's just what the hunter wants, of course – a fair chance sportingly taken.

But uplands are really just an amusing fancy. The real work, their real love, is in waterfowling. That's what they were bred for so long ago, and that's what pulls strongest at their hearts.

T hey are creatures of the water and the hunt; to deny this is to deny the dog his reason for being. Family dog? Of course. Companion? Certainly. Hunter? Always.

The taking of the makings of a duck dinner is not as important these days as it once was, and not as important as the companionship. For Labs love children and the mistresses of the house, but they hold dearest the unbreakable tie shared with the fellows who take them duck hunting.

No one ever accused a waterfowler of sanity, certainly no close relative by marriage, so it is not surprising to find that he always has near him a nearly lunatic black or yellow or chocolate dog in which not a tremor of doubt or fear ripples a wet, satin coat.

No water too big or cold or deep, no distance too far. For hunting Labs, there is only wave and wind and sky, and the shout of strong-hearted ancestors in their ears, urging them on.

W ith all that's been said of their
winsome ways and their ability
to love, we should stop once in
awhile to remember that there are few
creatures on earth as strong, courageous,
committed, and just plain tough as a
Labrador retriever.

These are not the eyes of a house dog nor a child's pet nor a fluff-bottomed hearth potato. Maybe at home tonight, but not here, not now.

PUPPIES!

Fun on the Run!

Those itchy, exploring teeth. Absolutely nothing, from anchor lines to aluminum siding, is safe. Those who take in their first Lab puppy find out early on that a dog who will one day lovingly handle a game bird with that soft, talented mouth will first commit untold atrocities with it as he learns how it's supposed to work.

Every owner thrills to the first time the inexplicable happens, when he sees the first bud of desire in his young friend to carry things to the master's hand.

Upon that simple act is built a lifetime union.

B ut before the training and the hunting and the discipline and the work, there are children to be alternately terrorized and charmed, a big new world to be explored, and a mother's devotion to be savored and remembered.

There comes a time early on when the bonding between you and your Lab really begins. It is the moment when the pup meets your eyes with a resolute gaze that says, simply, "I will trust you and do my best for you all the days of my life."